TURNING SORROW

SORROW

INTO

Song

TURNING
SORROW

INTO

Song

Devotional Thoughts For Those Who Grieve

by

JAN CARPENTER

Scripture Quotations are from the New American Standard Bible
© The Lockman Foundation 1960, 1962, 1963, 1968, 1971,
1972, 1973, 1975, 1977.
Used by permission.

Library of Congress Cataloging in Publication Data

Carpenter, Jan
  Turning Sorrow Into Song

I. Title

Library of Congress Catalog Card Number: 86-050542
ISBN   0-89066-081-6

Printed in U.S.A.

TABLE OF CONTENTS

INTRODUCTION

I have never known a time in my life when I did not believe in Christ. But merely believing wasn't enough. Circumstances in my life brought me face to face with the reality of death as I was forced to give two of my daughters back to the Father who had given them life.

In 1958, our five-year-old daughter Jody died suddenly from illness. I watched her life ebb away, powerless to prevent her death. Our daughter Melanie, born two years after Jody's death, lived until 1979 when at the age of nineteen, her life was snuffed out by a fatal automobile accident.

Both deaths were equally horrifying, but my response to each was totally different. Although I believed in Christ when Jody died, I had not allowed Him to be Lord of my life, to rule every aspect of my being. After losing Jody, I succumbed to twenty years of depression, insomnia, physical illnesses, constant medication, and emotional struggle.

Then we moved to a new area and a new church home, and some changes began to occur in my spiritual life. Through the loving influence of Christians around me, I was led into a close personal relationship with Jesus Christ. Four years before Melanie's death I was born again and began to grow in my spiritual life—and the resulting change in my emotional health and ability to cope quickly manifested itself.

Since the morning of Melanie's accident, I have known tremendous peace. With much gratitude—and a bit of surprise—I began to see the spiritual stability the Lord had been working in my life. And despite my sorrow and grief, He continues to lead me into new realms of growth. I certainly do not have all the answers, but I invite you to share my journey, realizing that together with Christ, we can make it through the most heartbreaking of circumstances.

I may not yet have begun to understand why my loved ones had to die, but I am convinced that God can bring meaning out of my sorrow. Although terrible and tragic, grief has purpose when relinquished to the Lord. In His mercy, He caresses our wounds with His balm and begins to heal us. In His mysterious way, He offers more than earthly life. And though His timing may seem strange, we have an opportunity to glorify Him, as we testify of His power and peace to others around us.

We cannot glorify the Lord without being blessed ourselves. Sorrow offered to Christ may be the greatest blessing of all!

—Jan Carpenter

PART ONE
Learning To Trust God And Others

1

The Song

Read Psalm 100

> *Serve the Lord with gladness; Come before him with joyful singing.* —*Psalm 100:2*

*T*he song and the listeners will vary. I may sing an aria to a vast audience or hum a brief lullaby to one tiny child. Sometimes the music is silent—an understanding glance, an "I care" smile, or an "I love you" hug.

Sometimes I am tempted to think that the length of my song or the size of my audience is important. But Jesus addressed crowds of thousands, and yet took time to minister life to one prostitute. Ninety-nine sheep were safe, but still He concerned Himself about the one lamb who was lost.

I must listen closely as the Maestro conducts. He is my flawless director, and lives will be touched as I sing in harmony with Him.

Dear Lord, thank you for the exquisite and powerful offering of song. Fix my eyes on you, my guide and director. Amen.

2

Infectious Trust

Read 2 Chronicles 20:20-25

> *Put your trust in the Lord, in the Lord your God, and you will be established. —2 Chronicles 20:20*

*W*hen Melanie's doctor diagnosed her cystic fibrosis, I cried uncontrollably.

"Knock off the tears," Dr. C. snapped. "You don't have time for that now. You have a lot to learn and a lot to do. Her life is in your hands."

Cruel and cutting as her words were, they did shock me into reality. Dr. C. had always given our children the finest care; often they would receive a tender kiss during an examination. Because of many dedicated doctors and nurses like her, Melanie had absolute trust in everybody. As far as she was concerned, they all loved her—and that's all she needed to know.

Because of her attitude, I made it through the next few years. Charting, administering vitamins and antibiotics, and pouring enzyme powder on everything she ate were all part of my daily routine. We made weekly visits to a local doctor and monthly visits to Dr. C. in Minneapolis.

Through it all, her huge eyes seemed to say, "It's all right, Mom. I know you are helping me." I learned to trust—mostly because Melanie did. Together, our trust sustained us until Melanie was declared completely healthy at three years old.

Thank you, God, for the faith of this precious child. Help me to learn to exercise childlike trust in you. Amen.

3

Ashes Into Garlands

Read Isaiah 61

> *To grant those who mourn in Zion, Giving them a garland instead of ashes . . . So they will be called oaks of righteousness, The planting of the Lord, that He may be glorified.* —Isaiah 61:3

*I*n addition to being sisters and best friends, Marie and I have still another bond, a bond that makes it possible for us to relate to one another at the deepest levels. I have suffered through the deaths of two children and she the deaths of two husbands.

Marie's first husband, Paul, died after 23 years of marriage; Roy, her second husband, died after twelve years together. Just as I did, she responded very differently to the second death.

Marie was shattered after Paul's death even though she believed in God. After hitting rock bottom, she made Christ the Lord of her life. Although Roy's death was as terrible as Paul's, my sister emerged with new strength, love, and a ministry of encouragement.

Neither of us would have chosen the chain of events that brought us into this special bond, but we treasure the bond. God embraces the broken, drawing them into His ministry of love.

Thank you, Lord, for bringing me through my sorrow. Help me to be your minister. Amen.

4

Receiving

Read John 13:1-20

> *Jesus answered him, "If I do not wash you, you have no part with Me."* —*John 13:8*

"*I*'ll make that molded salad that you like so much," said my friend Shirley, who was helping me prepare a second wedding reception for relatives who had been married in a far-off state. "But what else can I do for you?"

"Oh, thank you, but you don't need to do anything," I replied. "After all, you won't even be at the party."

"Okay, Jan," Shirley shot back, "but if you don't let me do this, you will never do another thing for me."

She was right. I made a practice of doing for others but when they wanted to "do" for me, my answer was always no. But receiving is just as important as giving. Without it, relationships are one-sided—both in human friendships and in my relationship with God.

I thank God for Shirley's anger. Without it, I might still be caught up in *doing* for my Savior without even having *received* Him into my heart.

Dear Heavenly Father, thank you for speaking to me through friends. Help me to listen. Amen.

5

Blessed With Delight

Read Psalm 37

> *Delight yourself in the Lord; And He will give you the desires of your heart.* —*Psalm 37:4*

I've known for some time that "my good works will not get me into heaven." But I usually feel that God loves me more when I am doing the "right thing."

One day I began to understand more clearly that nothing I can do will make Christ love me any more or any less. God didn't love Peter any less because he denied Him. And the Psalmist himself committed some grave acts of disobedience, yet God heralded David as a "man after My own heart." David knew how to enjoy the Lord.

I need to put aside "doing" and learn to love and delight in Him. He gives us hope; He picks us up when we fall; He forgives and forgives; He stands by us and loves us unconditionally and forever.

Thank you, Lord, for your faithfulness. Teach me to take time to be still and enjoy you. Amen.

6

The Image Of The Maker

Read Psalm 116:12-19

Precious in the sight of The Lord is the death of His godly ones. —Psalm 116:15

A fellow volunteer at the nursing home invited me to meet her father who lived there. When I entered his tiny room I noticed a large bulletin board tacked with family pictures. A *nice touch*, I thought, *but the room is still drab.* Then I turned to see a face lit up like a Christmas tree! Mr. Stubbs, in his nineties, was bedridden—but the restriction seemed of little importance to him.

Eyes shining, he sent me to the bulletin board while he lovingly pointed out his family members. "The Lord has been so good to me," he said. "Now I'm just waiting to go to glory. Hoped it was going to be the other night when my heart acted up again, but I guess it wasn't my time yet." Upon each of my visits, the same joyful face greeted me.

I shared his jubilation with his daughter one afternoon, and she remarked, "You know, Jan, we hadn't planned to display his body when he dies, but if he goes with that smile on his face, we're going to have to!"

This dear old gentleman's joy in Jesus transformed a tiny, drab room into a palace and rendered death a holy peace!

Dear God, thank you for the powerful testimony of this dear and gentle man. Make my life, like his, a reflection of your glory. Amen.

7

The Choice

Read Ephesians 4:25-32

Let all bitterness and wrath and anger and clamor and slander be put away from you, along with all malice. And be kind to one another, tender-hearted, forgiving each other, just as God in Christ also has forgiven you. —*Ephesians 4:31,32*

*W*e often stand at a crossroad with one pathway marked *forgiveness*, and the other marked *bitterness*. If we search hard enough, we always find someone or something to blame for the death of a loved one, personal tragedy, heartache, or failure.

Even Mary and Martha chided Jesus upon the death of Lazarus, each declaring, "Lord, if you had been here, my brother would not have died."

Although immediate blame is natural, continuing stubbornly down that road results only in bitterness. I see that bitterness in the eyes of a few people at the small nursing home I visit weekly. They will accept nothing—not my hand, not even my smile.

But others, like my friend Florence, do not give in to the destruction of bitterness. Florence's husband of twenty years walked out on her while, after suffering an aneurysm, she lay near death, comatose.

"At first I was bitter," confessed Florence. "And then I decided I was hurting myself most of all. I forgave my husband, and have never regretted it."

By forgiving, Florence made room for the joy of Christ which is now evident in her life. She chose forgiveness and saved herself from the destructive forces of bitterness and accusation.

Understanding Father, help me, like Florence, to choose forgiveness. Help me not to nurture my anger but to abandon it and rest in you. Thank you for forgiving me. Amen.

8

Euphemisms

Read John 14:1-6

> *Jesus said to him, "I am the way, and the truth, and the life; no one comes to the Father, but through Me."* —*John 14:6*

"*P*assed away"—although the phrase might be right for some, I am uneasy with it. "Died" is authentic—perhaps brutal—but at least I am forced to deal with it. A whispered "passed away" hardly seems real at all. It says to me, "Perhaps it didn't happen," or, "Put it aside and maybe it will go away."

Sympathy cards tell me, "He is just away," or "Beyond some rainbow," or even, "Whispering in the wind." But I have spent many difficult years learning to deal with reality, and I refuse to accept euphemisms, those dressed-up words served me in the name of comfort.

Our loved ones die. But because they die, they will live forever with Jesus Christ.

When I am positive about death, I can also be positive about life, for we must pass through both to enter eternity.

Lord, keep me from being judgmental when people are striving to help. And keep me in your truth that I might walk in your freedom. Amen.

9

God's Reconciling Love

Read 2 Timothy 4:5-8

But you, be sober in all things, endure hardship, do the work of an evangelist, fulfill your ministry.
—2 Timothy 4:5

When I first came to the small nursing home to which I am now committed, I was very uncomfortable. I didn't want to be there at all, yet I was drawn to return. It was clearly not my choice. Today the Lord Jesus has given me a love for my friends that I didn't think was possible. I leave with my heart full of joy.

We tend to believe that only pastors and "real church leaders" have calls from God. But God gives a ministry to every believer. We are God's reconciling love in the world.

The biblical leaders—Moses, Jeremiah, Peter, Paul—weren't leaders when God chose them. Most were simple people reluctant to be made into leaders. But God's choice is not always man's choice. The great men and women of biblical history changed the world through His reconciling love.

Make no mistake. We all have a ministry, a calling to reach out with hearts wide open to offer His love to those around us.

Thank you, Lord, for calling me into your service. Help me learn to show your love to others so that they might come to you. Amen.

10

Numbered Hairs

Read Matthew 10:29-31

Therefore do not fear; you are of more value than many sparrows. —Matthew 10:31

"**M**om, I'm more valuable than a sweater, right?" questioned my granddaughter, Carrie, as she arrived home from her second day of kindergarten. "I lost my sweater in school today," the small voice finished.

Although it was a pretty tricky way for Carrie to spring the loss on her mother, a something far more important lies in what she said. Carrie knows that she is valuable to her parents.

And I am of tremendous value to my Heavenly Father, no matter what mistakes I make. When I am lost, He leaves all the rest just to find me. He has knowledge of each falling sparrow, and He tells me that I am much more important than a sparrow. He counts each hair upon my head!

Most important of all, He sent Jesus to die to demonstrate the undeserved value that He places upon me!

Heavenly Father, thank you for placing value upon me. I love you. Amen.

11

Does Prayer Change Things?

Read 1 Peter 4:12-5:11

> *Rejoicing in hope, persevering in tribulation,
> devoted to prayer.* —Romans 12:12

"*P*rayer Changes Things," read the sticker on the dashboard of the car Melanie and I had shared—the one in which she was killed. When she fell asleep, the car struck the road divider and rolled end over end, finally landing upside down. Melanie survived the crash and hung onto life for another thirty hours, trapped in a prison of machines, never regaining consciousness.

Those thirty hours were both horrifying and wonderful. Although my daughter lay unconscious—perhaps dying—I knew without a doubt that God was in complete control. He visited us in the form of caring friends and relatives. He granted time for us to pray and lay hands on Melanie, telling her how much we loved her. He brought countless numbers of Melanie's friends to her side, people whose lives were touched—some transformed—by His work through her.

If prayer changes things, why, when I had prayed for Melanie that very morning, did God allow this to happen? If prayer changes things, why had we lost two children, while others around us seem to go untouched by tragedy?

I have no answers to these questions. But I can wait. I choose to trust my heavenly Father, who has better knowledge of my needs than I do. And I will continue to pray, to wait, and to depend upon Him.

Lord of comfort, thank you for your gift of prayer. Draw me close to you on difficult days. Remind me that when I least feel like praying, I need that time with you the most. Teach me to wait, to trust, to pray. Amen.

12

A Right Way To Pray?

Read Matthew 7:7-12

Ask, and it will be given to you; seek, and you will find; knock, and it will be opened to you.
                    —*Matthew 7:7*

*"**I**f we are Christians how can you not heal my daughter?' I confronted God." This was not my voice but that of a guest mother testifying on a Christian talk show. "Sometimes we forget to claim our rights as Christians," she went on, sharing that her daughter was healed completely.

"Hey!" I yelled at the T.V. "I'm a Christian too, and *my* daughters died. Are you telling me that if I had prayed differently, with more authority, my girls would be alive?"

Of course not. The woman had every right to be ecstatic about her daughter's recovery, but many people are misled and hurt by such a statement.

All of us are confronted with doubts from time to time, but God doesn't say He answers only particular prayers. He says He answers *all* prayers. We know He answered our prayers when Melanie was in her coma, and the reason she died was definitely not because we didn't pray right.

Only God knows the reason why. What I know is that He never left our side. His presence with us was overwhelming at her death as was His assurance that He had taken her in love.

Lord, protect us from thoughtless statements, and keep us forgiving those who seem to have quick and easy answers. Amen.

PART TWO
Hearing The Note Of Compassion

13

In The Dark Of The Night

Read Luke 22:39-46

Now an angel from heaven appeared to Him, strengthening Him. —Luke 22:43

*I*n Africa, I am told, grows a cactus called the cereus. It's not particularly beautiful, with spread-eagle broad leaves and multiple stems. Then it buds, and four weeks later a gorgeous flower bursts forth with a magnificent fragrance. But the flowering only happens in the black of night.

During my black night, I continued to believe in God, and I wanted very much for Him to approve of me. I tried to do everything I could to please Him.

Father Ryan, the pastor of the church that our family eventually joined, reached out to us. Jim phoned him the morning of Jody's death and he was at our door in a matter of minutes. He got the children's breakfast and perked a pot of coffee for the three of us. As Father Ryan continued his visits daily for more than two weeks, I realized that God sent us His love through this dear, compassionate friend.

As I struggled with recurrent fears, Father Ryan continued to minister to me, making certain that members of the church reached out to welcome me in. Out of my own black night, nurtured by Father Ryan's love, the flower of my cactus slowly began to blossom, offering me a ray of hope.

When life is most difficult, Lord, help me recognize those you have sent to me. When life is joyful, help me minister to those who endure their own dark nights. Amen.

14

Free To Fail

Read Galatians 4:28-31

It was for freedom that Christ set us free: therefore keep standing firm and do not be subject again to a yoke of slavery. —Galatians 5:1

*E*arly one morning, I was thinking, thanking God for the members of my church. They sense when I am down; they are fun to be with; they are encouraging, and their very presence offers comfort.

"Why, Lord," I asked, "are those people such a blessing to me?" Then I realized that with my church family I am free to fail. If I overlook a detail while earnestly setting up the altar, nobody gets upset. If I muddle up while delivering a speech, no one condemns me. Each member is free to be an individual.

Jesus said, "I have come to set you free"—free to be all He intended me to be; free to "sing my song."

When I stumble or even fall, my church family is there to take my hand or to pick me up again. They don't love me any less because I am imperfect—in fact, their love grows stronger.

Thank you, Lord, for those who give me the freedom to fail. Help me to be as generous to them; let me learn to live by your grace. Amen.

15

Family Ties

Read Matthew 6:19-21

> *For where your treasure is, there will your heart be also.*
> —*Matthew 6:21*

*A*t a Christian Writers' conference, I had the privilege of meeting Joseph Bayly. Seated on stage with a panel of fellow writers, each began to describe his "writing office" and working conditions.

One young man, creating out of his home, described how he locked out his family when he intended to work. As professionals, he explained very strongly, we have that right.

With obvious hurt in his eyes, Mr. Bayly waited his turn. "God forbid," he said then, "that I be in the ministry of helping others and shut out my own family in the process."

Joe Bayly and his wife have buried three children. He knows the value of his family, and he treasures them. In his book *The Last Thing We Talk About*, Bayly shares his feelings and experiences arising out of the death of those three sons.

Thank you, Lord, for people who set a quality example of how I am to love my family, your gift to me. Help me never to take them for granted or let my own work interfere with my appreciation of them. Amen.

16

Shared Sorrow

Read Hebrews 13:12-16

And do not neglect doing good and sharing; for with such sacrifices God is pleased.
—*Hebrews 13:16*

*O*ne Wednesday morning my friend Susan admired the pink shirt I was wearing. When I told her that it had belonged to Melanie, she said, "Oh, doesn't it feel good?"

I was astounded by her ability to know exactly how I felt. Then she held up a leather handbag, explaining that it had been her mother's. Susan's mother had died several years before from cancer.

The Swedish say, "SHARED JOY IS A DOUBLE JOY, AND SHARED SORROW IS HALF THE SORROW." That saying became real for Susan and me one particular Wednesday morning!

Dear Lord, keep me open to sharing our sorrow as well as joys. Amen.

17

A Friend Indeed!

Read John 15:12-17

A friend loves at all times. —*Proverbs 17:17*

*T*wo fragile fuzzy ducklings huddle lovingly together in a vast sunny patch of marigolds. The caption on my husband's poster reads, "A friend is someone who knows everything about you and still loves you."

In the sorrow over the death of our children, Jim and I have experienced the unvarnished meaning of friendship. He has breathed comfort into us through our friends, but we have learned that we cannot burden them by expecting perfection when there is only one Perfect Friend.

Time and again, human friends disappoint us. But Jesus Christ is the Absolute Friend. He knows all our uncleanness but chooses to see us with His heart rather than His eyes.

Thank you, dear Lord, for friendship. Help me to know that to have a friend, I must be one. Amen.

18

A New Boldness

Read Hebrews 4:13-16

Let us therefore draw near with confidence to the throne of grace, that we might receive mercy and may find grace to help us in time of need.

—Hebrews 4:16

*T*wo years ago, I was hurt and angry because my pastor hadn't paid me a visit after my serious surgery—a ridiculous attitude, because although we were close, I had not even mentioned that I was going into the hospital. Foolishly, I expected him to read my mind.

The other day a friend admired my "courage to ask for assistance when the going gets rough." I have even surprised myself with my boldness. Perhaps it springs from desperation.

Even though it seems obvious to us that we need help and comfort, we must not always wait for others to make that first move. Our requests for help afford others the opportunity to serve!

Thank you, Lord, for helping hands and helping hearts. Teach me to humble myself and seek assistance from your people. Amen.

19

The Need For Extravagance

Read Luke 7:36-50

And standing behind Him at His feet,
weeping, she began to wet His feet with her tears, and
wiped them with the hair of her head, and kissed His
feet, and anointed them with the ointment.

—Luke 7:38

I haven't always approved of this woman. I had no problem with her sin or her tears, but the extravagance of the perfume was difficult to accept. There *are* always the starving masses to feed.

The world's pain deepens as the "Be good to yourself" and "Do your own thing" philosophy continues. Loneliness is all around. Human need has never been more crucial. Extravagant as it may seem, we need to smash our alabaster jars and rain the sweet ointment of Christ's love on God's people.

Dear Lord Jesus, help me to be extravagant in my love for others. Amen.

20

Listening

Read Mark 4:1-24

And He was saying to them, "Take care what you listen to; by your standard of measure it shall be measured to you; and more shall be given you besides." —Mark 4:24

Within each of us lies a deep-rooted need to speak of the one we've lost, almost as if we might smother if we don't find someone to listen. That need peaks when the funeral service has ended and everyone else goes on with life. The world can't stop, but oh, how we wish it could at least slow down!

When our first daughter, Jody, died suddenly, I felt alone and abandoned. We had moved to a small town just two short months before her death. Jim was working 14 hours a day, so in addition to missing Jody, I yearned for the company of an adult.

One morning I met a young mother at a club meeting. A few days later she invited me to her home for a cup of coffee. With tears brimming, but a tiny bit of hope inside, I shakily made my way to her door.

She took my coat, invited me to sit down, and surprised me by offering a short prayer before coffee.

"Jan, I'm not sure what to do for you," she said. "Do you want to talk about Jody, or would you rather avoid the subject for now?"

Five tear-soaked tissues later I began telling her everything that was stored in my heart—everything from my loneliness for Jody to the special horrors of arranging a funeral for such a little girl.

A series of shared coffees followed, with one common denominator: my new friend always listened.

Father, help me to listen to others. And thank you for those who listen to me. Amen.

21

The Servant

Read John 13:5-17

If I then, the Lord and the Teacher washed your feet, you also ought to wash one another's feet.
                                        —*John 13:14*

*T*wo weeks after Melanie's death, I had an appointment with a general practitioner whom I had not met. Not anxious to strike up a new relationship, I wanted to stay home, but since I am not one to break an appointment, I literally drove myself to his office.

During the examination he asked about my family, and I told him of Melanie's fatal accident and also of Jody's sudden death. Stunned, he remarked quietly, "That must be the worst thing that could ever happen to anybody."

After a period of silence, he finished the examination by looking compassionately at my calloused feet. "My," he exclaimed, "they look sore! I tell you what— I have some extra time today. How about if we give your feet a hot bath, and then I can work on your callouses?" I remembered my Lord's ministry to His disciples; amazed, I sat quietly and received the ministry of one who had His servant heart.

Caring Lord, I know it was you and I am deeply grateful. Help me to see you in those who minister your love. Amen.

22

Choosing The "Good Part"

Read Luke 10:38-42

And she had a sister called Mary, who moreover was listening to the Lord's word, seated at His feet.   —Luke 10:39

*D*ear Mike,
   I know how hard it is to lose someone you love, but I found that time is the best healer. If you ever need a friend or someone to talk to, please keep me in mind. I'll always be here.

Love,
Melanie

   I discovered this buried treasure just yesterday when I decided to clean a closet and let go of more of Melanie's possessions. I cried hard, but I also understood my daughter's sensitivity in a new light.

   Although Melanie was only in her early teens, she had already learned through her own suffering the important ingredients of healing. Time is indeed curative, and the friend who will listen is of utmost significance. But I suspect that she had also learned that reaching out to others was vital to her own good health.

   Jesus knew the real value of time. He never rushed about or jumped into things. Not only was He a listener, He treasured and cherished those around Him who were. Mary sat at the feet of Jesus, listening intently to His every word, while Martha scurried about them. Jesus commended her: "Mary has chosen the good part which shall not be taken away from her."

   Father, thank you for moments of quietness, for the healing brought by time and love. Help me to sit at your feet, to "choose the better part." Amen.

PART THREE
Responding To Hope

23

Marshmallow Pumpkins

Read Romans 8:28-39

> *For I am convinced that neither death nor life, nor angels, nor principalities, nor things present nor things to come, nor powers, nor height nor depth, nor any other created thing, shall be able to separate us from the love of God which is [found] in Christ Jesus our Lord.* —Romans 8:38,39

*I*t was my first time out since Melanie's death. I needed to go grocery shopping, but I felt so fragile that I wanted to hang a sign around my neck reading, "Please be kind to me—my daughter has been killed, and we used to do this together."

The market was bustling with shoppers and my cart was almost filled. Then I spotted the marshmallow pumpkins—Melanie's favorites—and burst immediately into tears. Even as a teenager, Melanie would giggle with delight when I brought them home to her. Halloween was approaching; of course they would be on display! I wanted to desert my groceries and run out of the store. Why hadn't I remained at home where it was safe?

But an astonishing peace swept over me as this thought came to mind: "There is no *unsafe* for the Christian. All is safe in Christ Jesus."

With hope renewed I pushed my cart into the next aisle.

Dear Heavenly Father, instill a constant hope in my heart that will bring me through my loneliness and shine for those around me. Amen.

24

It's Up To Me

Read Proverbs 15:13-15

> *All the days of the afflicted are bad, But a cheerful heart has a continual feast.* —*Proverbs 15:15*

"The tiny chickadee is the most cheerful of all birds" according to my bird book. When a variety of birds feast at our backyard feeder, the chickadees stand out.

Nothing seems to dampen their spirit as they sing their way through wind and rain. The swirling snow of Minnesota winters only encourages the flock as they dart about, making the feeder look like a busy airport.

This morning while sleepily fumbling about my kitchen, reluctantly cleaning up after last night's dinner party, I thought, *I can be like the chickadee! I don't have to be grumpy or sad. I have a choice. It's up to me!* Flashing a smile, I spoke words of encouragement to my husband, Jim, as he left home to start his day's work.

Cheerfulness is contagious. My little feathered friend's attitude is beginning to rub off on me! I do have a choice—and I can choose His way.

Thank you, God, for the many ways you encourage me. Help me to pass it on. Amen.

25

A Fresh Start

Read Psalm 30:1-5

Weeping may last for the night, But a shout of joy comes in the morning. —*Psalm 30:5b*

What a rotten day! Nothing went right. And it all began *before* I had one sip of my morning coffee.

First I stubbed my little toe on the post of the bed. Then came a distressing phone call. And because my arthritis was exceptionally painful I whined all morning, depressing myself as much as everyone around me.

While I was canning in the afternoon, a quart jar exploded, shooting tomato juice all over the kitchen, hitting my freshly laundered curtains dead center. I sat right down on the floor and cried.

Desiring to accomplish something for the day, I began writing an article. But after tearing up five sheets of words that wouldn't come together, I quit. By evening I was exhausted and decided to go to bed early. Searching for something to be thankful for as I said goodnight to the Lord, I suddenly remembered a friend's commentary on her bad day: "I can hardly wait to go to bed so that I can get up tomorrow morning and start fresh, all over again!"

Thank you, Lord, for my friend's words and for fresh, new starts. I love you, Lord. Amen.

26

Never Again!

Read Revelation 21:1-7

> *And He shall wipe away every tear from their eyes: and there shall no longer be any death: there shall no longer be any mourning, or crying, or pain; the first things have passed away.* —*Revelation 21:4*

*A*s I grow older, I get more and more excited about the second coming of Jesus Christ. Scriptures that tell of that great event to come make my heart soar. Songs that herald its arrival bring a smile to my face.

All the pain which has become such a difficult part of my life these past few years will be gone! Crying and sadness, a fragment of each day on this earth, shall vanish! We will celebrate with the heavenly hosts and our hosannas will ring down the streets of gold. Jesus, King of Kings, will be present in all His glory.

There will be a joyous reunion for me with Jody and Melanie and all our loved ones. Together we will hug and talk and laugh and sing. But best of all, we will never have to say goodbye again!

Thank you, Heavenly Father, for the beautiful expectation of heaven. Amen.

27

Hope

Read Romans 5:1-11

> *And hope does not disappoint, because the love of God has been poured out within our hearts through the Holy Spirit who was given to us.*
>
> *—Romans 5:5*

*I*t was a grey, bleak, Good Friday morning! My pastor and I had come to share a Communion breakfast with our friends at the small nursing home.

Just as we were finishing our last sip of coffee and the service was about to begin, Pastor Jim leaned over and asked in a whisper, "Jan, will you share what Jesus means in your life?"

"Sure!" I answered boldly, while inside I was trembling. I had been ill and felt especially weak and helpless this particular morning. What could I possibly say that might bring hope to these people?

All eyes searched mine as I stood up to speak. I looked back and saw their hurts and their handicaps, and my heart sank. Then, unexpected excitement rose in my heart as I began. "Hope," I said. "Jesus Christ means hope; this home is temporary. Just think, we will have mansions in heaven! There will be no more wheelchairs and no more walkers, no more sickness and no more pain. Jesus Christ is the hope of a new, eternal life!"

HOPE

Without hope,
Eyes become vacant;
Shoulders droop;
Nerves jangle;
Lines appear on faces, frowns take over;
Bodies become tired and heavy;
Sickness prevails;
Mornings are unbearable, and sleep is my only friend.

With hope,
Eyes light up;
Shoulders straighten;
Nerves quiet;
Lines disappear;
Frowns turn right side up to form smiles;
Bodies become light and health dominates;

Mornings are welcome, and sleep is a waste as time
    becomes precious.
Jesus Christ offers the only lasting hope.

—Jan Carpenter

*Heavenly Father, we thank you, for the offering of
hope in your Son Jesus Christ. Help us to offer Him to
others. Amen.*

28

Waterproof Wednesdays

Read Jeremiah 8:18-22

> *Is there no balm in Gilead? Is there no physician there? Why then has not the health of the daughter of my people been restored?* —*Jeremiah 8:22*

A miraculous midweek balm is applied to me every Wednesday morning. This balm, the healing touch of Jesus, places my problems in the right perspective, soothing my broken heart as well as my physical pain. Sometimes I pray as well that it will ease a family member's pain or help a friend in trouble.

The balm is offered at a Holy Communion and healing service held in our small A-framed church. Following intercessory prayer and Communion, our pastor invites anyone who desires healing to come for prayer and laying on of hands.

The sweet ointment, present throughout the entire service, is now most generously applied. When tears precede release and healing, we always have a box of tissues within reach. And I always wear waterproof mascara on Wednesday mornings.

Sometimes only three or four people come to receive what Jesus offers, but that doesn't seem to matter to Him. He is always there applying the balm!

Thank you, Lord, for your strengthening provisions. Help me to pass them on. Amen.

29

Because I Believe

Read 2 Peter 1:1-15

For by these He has granted to us His precious and magnificent promises, in order that by them you might become partakers of the divine nature, having escaped the corruption that is in the world by lust.
—2 Peter 1:4

A recent funeral I attended caused me great frustration. The service was held in a magnificent old church with exquisite flowers and wonderful musical selections. The pastor spoke the expected words, and the crowd listened attentively. Every detail was carefully thought out. Yet the whole funeral was bleak and empty.

What was wrong? Why did I feel so frustrated? Not one person sounded as though he believed a single word of what was said or sung!

My heart raced. I wanted to dash to the front of the church and scream, "It's true! All of it is true. God keeps His promises. He WILL raise us up on the last day. And then we will see Him and He will be surrounded by our loved ones!"

I kept quiet, of course. But I went home thankful that I knew the truth about God's promises for the future.

Heavenly Father, thank you for your promises. Help me to sing my song because I believe it. Amen.

30

Forever

Read Psalm 16

Thou wilt make known to me the path of life; In thy presence is fullness of joy; In thy right hand there are pleasures forever. —*Psalm 16:11*

*O*ne beautiful, vibrant fall day I became sad and lonely. I longed for Melanie to throw her arms around me and silently place her head upon my shoulder as she had done so many times.

The sorrows of the past two years paraded across my mind—loss of my daughter, loss of my mother, and even the loss of my precious country home. "Losses and changes! I HATE them!" I shouted aloud. "Doesn't anything worthwhile ever last?"

Nothing is forever, I decided silently, fighting back the tears. As I reluctantly pulled into my church parking lot, I spotted my friend Eva. She walked over to my car and handed a note through the window. In spite of myself, a smile crossed my face as I read it. After signing her name, she had added, "Your friend forever."

"Hallelujah!" I sang. "We ARE forever. Christians are forever."

Loving God, thank you for making forever *possible through the death of your Son Jesus Christ. Amen.*

PART FOUR
Discovering New Life In Christ

31

For Real

Read Psalm 15

> *O Lord, who may abide in Thy tent? Who may dwell on Thy holy hill? He who walks with integrity, and works righteousness, and speaks truth in his heart.* —Psalm 15:1-2

*M*y friend Bruce introduced me at our annual church dinner so I could present my outreach report. "She's for real," he said in closing.

She hasn't always been, I thought to myself. *In fact, she was downright phony.*

How we come across to others in the hope that they will like us is important to everyone, but to me it became a top priority, taking precedence over reality. I was pretty well liked by everybody but myself, but no one really knew what I stood for. Trying to side with everybody made me pretty insipid.

I really did care about people, but I was a bit mixed up in how I acted out that caring. I tried not to disagree with anyone—after all, wasn't that what Paul meant when he said he was all things to all people?

When I began to allow the Lord to rule my life, I began to change. I started to see myself as God does, and He showed me that being genuine was being positive about myself as well as others. My self-esteem began to climb.

During and after Melanie's death I learned much about being real. How could anyone help me if I pretended I was always fine? How could I find comfort if I pretended I didn't need any?

And most importantly, how could God help me if I tried to deceive Him by hiding my real emotions? He knows them anyway, but He won't push His way in to help.

Being real with God has transformed my life. As I began to be open with Him, I found the freedom to be real with others.

Lord, thank you for setting me free through reality. Amen.

32

Christ Is Born!

Read Luke 2:1-20

> *And she gave birth to her firstborn son; and she wrapped Him in cloths and laid Him in a manger, because there was no room for them in the inn.*
> *—Luke 2:7*

*E*xcept for the beautiful candlelight church service, Christmas Eve was awful, especially since Melanie's death five years ago. If only we could all talk about how empty life is without her, how we miss her robust enthusiasm and hearty laughter! But we don't. Instead we clench our teeth, determined to enjoy ourselves, and we end up angry and hurt.

I escaped into bed when it was all over, anxious to shut out all the hurts. Sleep came only after hard sobbing and an ice pack for the resulting headache. "Please, God, make tomorrow better," I pleaded.

Early Christmas morning I awoke and made my way to the kitchen. As I peered out the window at the snowy bird feeder, chickadees and black-eyed juncos were scurrying about, happily enjoying an early feeding. The Christmas wreath I had hung at the top provided additional delight as they darted back and forth nestling into its soft greens.

I began to prepare a cherry coffeecake, when a feeling of warmth came over me, as though I were being hugged. An unmistakable peace settled upon me as I thought of Jesus' birth. Christmas Eve was certainly frustrating for Joseph and Mary. She was about to deliver a baby and there wasn't even a bed for her to rest her weary body on. Nobody else even cared! But with the miracle and majesty of Jesus' birth, the pain and frustration lost its importance. And as that birth became real to me, the frustration and pain of last night were gone, and the beauty of this day was all that mattered.

I still don't have any real answers about Christmas Eve, and I don't know what next year will bring, but I do know one thing: God understands our sorrows and He cares.

Heavenly Father, thank you for the birth of your Son and His knowledge of human sorrow. Thank you for our family. Amen.

33

God's Power

Read Ruth 1:1-17

> *Where you die, I will die, and there I will be*
> *buried . . .* —Ruth 1:17

"*T*hank you, Lord, that I am no longer the same person!*"

Two weeks after Jody's death, I screamed out the window, "Why are you all going on with your lives as though nothing has happened? Don't you realize that my Jody is dead?" I wished that the world would stop.

There are many days following Jody's death that I still can't recall. Jim had to take Debbie and Jamie to our babysitter's home at times when I was out of control.

I continued to have difficulty eating and sleeping despite the expensive and potent tranquilizers and sleeping pills I was taking. I developed chronic bronchitis and had to have more medication and constant vaporizing.

I was seized with attacks of fear. Sometimes I would leave church before the service was over. Frequently I ran from the market, leaving behind a basket full of groceries. Although my Bible lay open on the coffee table, I was unable to concentrate long enough to read it. When I became afraid to leave my house, I begged my psychiatrist to administer shock treatments.

After a consultation, my doctors decided that not eating was my way of committing suicide. Perhaps I was punishing myself so that I might suffer as I had seen Jody suffer before she died. What difference did it make? I still couldn't bring her back.

But the very morning of Melanie's funeral, I drove myself to the church to set up the communion altar linens that a friend had sewn and dedicated to Melanie's memory. The day before, I had selected all of the music and had arranged for every detail of the service, making sure that it would carry the theme of joy and celebration that I had insisted upon. I felt great joy at her funeral and, in spite of many lonely times, I continue to know His joy.

Lord, I am in awe of your power. Thank you for your grace and your mercy, and for never giving up on me. Amen.

34

The Return Of
The Good Samaritan

Read Luke 10:29-37

But a certain Samaritan . . . came to him and bandaged up his wounds, pouring oil and wine on them. —Luke 10:33,34

*M*y daughter, Debbie, was hurrying home from the market with the week's supply of groceries when her car stopped dead! Three-year-old Sarah was along, there wasn't a service station in sight, and five-year-old Carrie was waiting to be picked up at nursery school.

Deep in contemplation as to what her next move might be, Debbie was startled when a young man poked his head through the car window. "Are you all right?" he questioned.

Debbie explained her predicament, and the young man quickly crawled under her car, with only a stick for a tool.

In a short time he climbed back out, scrambled into the driver's seat and started up the motor. "You should be okay now," he announced with a wide smile.

Noticing the expression on my daughter's face as she surveyed his white trousers now covered with black dirt, the young man exclaimed, "You're wondering why I did this? It's because Jesus did so much for me!"

Dear Lord Jesus, thank you for the boldness of this young man. Help me to be as bold   both in words and in action. Amen.

35

Step Out

Read Jeremiah 1:4-10

> *Do not be afraid of them, For I am with you to deliver you, declares the Lord.* —*Jeremiah 1:8*

*S*hortly after my renewal in Christ, I was asked to be a member of the board that governs our church. "Don't give us your answer now, Jan," our pastor urged, "first pray about it."

My mind raced back to my previous church, where the same invitation was extended. I was too busy, I claimed. The truth was, I had rejected a variety of opportunities from time to time fearing that they were over my head. I was always comfortable working one-on-one with people, but the thought of being an overseer was scary—even though I loved the idea of the importance that it might afford me.

This time, although I still clung to some of the same fears, I was beginning to see what the Lord could accomplish if I made myself available. Through prayer, I was led to read Jeremiah's call from God. "I do not know how to speak, Lord God," the prophet answered. Then the Lord stretched out His hand and touched Jeremiah's mouth, saying, "Behold, I have put my words in your mouth."

That promise is not only for Jeremiah, nor is it only for me. It is for each child of God who in faith steps out beyond his own competence and looks to God's omnipotence.

Thank you, Lord Jesus, for turning my weakness into strength. Help me to respond in faith to you. Amen.

36

No Wonder

Read Luke 5:1-11

And He got into one of the boats . . . and began teaching . . . And when He had finished speaking, He said to Simon, "Put out into the deep water and let down your nets for a catch."

—Luke 5:3,4

*J*im and I were on our way up north to join friends for a week-end at their lake cabin, a three-hour drive. After an extraordinarily busy week, we were both eager to unwind.

Arriving at the cabin, we greeted Bob and Betty with the usual hugs. After unpacking our clothes and putting away the groceries, we decided to postpone dinner a bit and get some early fishing in.

We chose to try our chance in a small channel on the opposite side of the lake. Frogs croaked on distant lily pads. The tall birch trees swayed in a soft wind and glistened in the sunset waters. Our boat rocked gently, almost still.

"No wonder Jesus spent so much time on the water!" I blurted out, breaking the silence. Everyone looked surprised, then smiled.

Jesus knows all my thoughts and feelings, I mused. But it had never dawned on me that I could know any of His. What a joy to realize His need for rest and refreshment as He has always known mine!

Thank you, Lord, for providing times of refreshment. Stop me when I overdo on my own. Amen.

37

Keep It Simple

Read Psalm 19

The testimony of the Lord is sure, making wise the simple. —Psalm 19:7

*R*ecently, I attended an afternoon symphony with my son Jamie, who shares my appreciation of music. Arriving early, we took our places and peered around the concert hall. A vast assortment of people began claiming their seats. Behind us was a young couple with two lively children, and in front of us sat an elderly bearded gentleman. Many students were in the audience, some dressed up, others in blue jeans.

A symphony concert can be enjoyed by all people no matter what their training or background. The same is true of the gospel of Jesus Christ. But sometimes we complicate it.

Often we tend to change it, perhaps trying to give it some sophistication. Other times we alter its message to fit the situation and perhaps not embarrass anyone.

The gospel of Jesus Christ applies to all people, of all educational and occupational backgrounds. The Word of Christ is simple, available to everyone.

Dear Heavenly Father, thank you for your simple message. Help me not to complicate it, but to demonstrate it. Amen.

38

"To Sleep: Perchance To Dream...

Read Psalm 126

When the Lord brought back the captive ones of Zion, we were like those who dream. —Psalm 126:1

"**A**y, there's the rub!" says Shakespeare's character Hamlet. After the death of a loved one, falling asleep is difficult. But even worse is waking up abruptly to a pounding heart and the horrifying truth: *My loved one really did die! This was no dream.*

I can clearly remember, even though it was so many years ago, how I tried to stay awake after Jody died, so I could avoid that terrible startling awareness. I felt as though it would never end.

I was also afraid I might dream about her. Sometimes she would beckon to me, telling me she was still alive. Other times I would see her suffering and dying all over again.

But since Melanie's death, something wonderful has occurred during my sleep. Although I have no explanation and am unable to recall any details, I have awakened fresh in the morning with a feeling of contentment, as though I have spent a most enjoyable time with Melanie.

As distressing as some of our dreams are, they can serve a purpose, releasing us from undesirable fears and emotions. And God can use them for His purposes, to draw us close to Him.

Lord, help me remember that everything that happens in my life has purpose. Amen.

39

God's Paradox

Read 2 Corinthians 12:7-10

> *Therefore I am well content with weaknesses, with insults, with distresses, with persecutions, with difficulties, for Christ's sake; for when I am weak, then I am strong.* —2 Corinthians 12:10

"Why do I continue feeling as though God views me as special when I am so angry with Him for allowing Gary to be killed?" questioned my dear friend, Jean. She and her husband, Mark, were visting us shortly after their son had died in a motorcycle tragedy.

Months later I was to experience an overwhelming abundance of God's love as I stood at the foot of my daughter Melanie's bed after her death. Never had I felt more confident of the reality of resurrection. God's presence was overpowering.

As Christians, we live in a world of paradox. Paul offered our Lord his highest praises while chained in a dank prison. Job, while afflicted, declared, "God does great and unsearchable things." As we submit to His transforming power, circumstances hold little importance to us. When we are the weakest, Christ is the strongest.

Dear Jesus, help me to remember how very much you love me, that your love can penetrate any difficulty. Thank you for making blessed times out of difficult times. Amen.

40

Sweet Sadness

Read Jude 17-25

Now to Him who is able to keep you from stumbling, and to make you stand in the presence of His glory blameless with great joy. —Jude 24

*M*ore than anything else I can imagine, I would love to have my two girls back. Even though I have learned to live and even laugh again, there will always be a longing in my heart for them. But out of that sadness there flourishes a sweetness, an intimacy with Jesus.

Knowing I can't make it on my own, I must depend upon Him. True, there are times when I think He has forgotten about me. But then He comes, once more, pushing back the circumstances and making nothing else seem important beside His incomparable presence.

The joy and sweetness of Jesus does not come cheap; the price for me has been the wounds and bruises of my heart. But though the cost is high, the investment is worth the risk; in return I gain the priceless riches of Christ's glory.

Lord Jesus, I adore you. You mean more to me than anyone or anything. Help me to keep you first in my life. Amen.

41

Outer And Inner

Read 2 Corinthians 4:11-18

*Therefore we do not lose heart, but though
our outer man is decaying, yet our inner man is being
renewed day by day.*   —*2 Corinthians 4:16*

I celebrated my fifty-sixth birthday in May. My head says, "That's not possible," while the rest of my body quickly argues, "Oh, yes, it is!"

Arthritis has rendered me a little unsteady; I now must be careful that I don't fall. This winter, instead of sliding on icy puddles as I used to do, I will probably avoid them altogether.

I can't eat the foods I used to love; almost everything has some kind of unfriendly effect upon my system.

My weight is slowly rising, distributing itself unequally around my middle.

I never sleep through a night anymore; lines and wrinkles are beginning to appear.

Growing old isn't very easy, but life is getting better. *My inner self is renewing!* And rather than worrying about trivia, I'm learning what is really important.

I'm not trying to change anybody else these days; I'm finding it much easier to love people where they are.

Not only do I smell more flowers today, I can identify most of them. Now and then someone asks me for advice, and I find that I am wiser than I used to be. Most of all, I am learning to change what I can and accept what I can't.

My outer body is slowly and surely decaying but my inner person is growing stronger in the peace that Christ offers to those who trust in Him.

Lord, you are true to your word. Help me to be true to mine. Amen.

PART FIVE
Praise In The Midst Of Pain

42

The Advantages Of
A Broken Heart

Read Psalm 34

The Lord is near to the brokenhearted, and saves those who are crushed in spirit. —*Psalm 34:18*

"*I*t's the heart afraid of breaking that never learns to dance," proclaimed the voice on the radio. "That's it!" I shouted. "That explains it!" I hurt now more than ever, but that same hurt contains many blessings as well.

My heart is broken and won't be mended until I am reunited with my girls. But pain is not necessarily bad. I accept my brokenness.

Doctors tell me that a sprain can be more painful than a break. It's the same way with the heart. If I stiffen up and struggle to keep my heart intact, the pain will hurt much more than if I relax and let it break.

Jesus' heart was continually broken, by His own choice. When we allow the same to happen to us, we are yielding to Christ. Only then will our song become marked with His love, and our broken hearts a blessing.

Heavenly Father, teach my heart how to dance for you. Amen.

43

Forsaken?

Read 2 Corinthians 4:1-18

We are afflicted in every way, . . . persecuted, but not forsaken; struck down, but not destroyed.
—2 Corinthians 4:8,9

I've had many difficult days, days when I feel alone and unimportant. God seems far away and I wonder if He has forgotten about me. But I've learned not to give up! It *is* always the darkest before the dawn, and joy *does* come in the morning. I stand on a brink—a brink that might just as well be one of joy as one of sorrow.

There are no easy answers. But Jesus knows my despair, for even He cried out as He hung on the cross, "My God, my God, why hast thou forsaken me?"

Life is painful, but we can learn to grow from our pain if we don't cling to it. Then we can stand up and sing, even if the song includes tears!

Dear Heavenly Father, pour your healing love on your sorrowing servant. Thank you for allowing us to know that you felt forsaken too. Amen.

44

"Oh, No!"

Read 1 Peter 5:8-11

Be sober, be vigilant; because your adversary the devil walks about like a roaring lion, seeking whom he may devour. —1 Peter 5:8

I wanted to have another child immediately after Jody's death, but my doctors didn't think it was a good idea. They advised me to wait a year, then reconsider. Melanie was born a little over two years later on July 10, 1960.

All during my pregnancy I longed for a girl—so much that I was ashamed of myself. I didn't expect her to replace Jody, but I wanted another little girl.

Our doctor allowed Jim into the delivery room right after Melanie was born. He was the first person to hold her. We could hardly wait to bring their new sister home to Debbie and Jamie.

"Is everything all right with my baby?" I questioned Dr. P. one day while I was in the hospital. "She has so much mucous in her system."

"Jan, that just happens sometimes after birth. She'll be okay," he reassured me.

When she was nine months old, on our physician's advice, we brought Melanie back to Minneapolis, to be examined by our former pediatrician. Her body was still producing abnormal amounts of mucous, and in spite of her ravenous appetite, she was underweight.

After examining Melanie, Dr. C. requested that she be hospitalized for tests. She suspected cystic fibrosis, an incurable disease. Melanie had all the symptoms but one: she was not irritable as most C.F. children are.

For nine days Melanie smiled her way through tests. Nothing dampened her spirits—not the needle, not even the warm plastic bag that covered everything but her head and was designed to measure and examine her sweat.

Finally on the ninth day, with my whole body trembling, I faced Dr. C. "We are sure," she said, looking directly into my eyes, "that Melanie has cystic fibrosis."

"God, You can't!!! I've already lost one child!" I shouted. But it was true. And even through that dark night of pain, the Lord met us, sustained us, and showed us His will.

Lord, help me to trust you in my times of pain and despair. Help me remember that nothing comes to me except through your hand. Amen.

45

Not On This Earth

Read Isaiah 11:1-10

> *He . . . will decide with fairness for the afflicted of the earth.*   —*Isaiah 11:4b*

"*I*t's not fair!" My children complain—and I have said it, too. Life upon this earth is, indeed, not fair. Coping is much simpler for me when I can accept that. If I do not, then I search for ways to blame myself when I shouldn't.

Of course we suffer as a result of our own mistakes and wrong choices, but most of us know grief that goes far beyond that. Job, for example, did not deserve the devastation that came upon him, because the Lord declared that there was no one like him upon all the earth.

God does allow unfair suffering in this world, but we can take heart. If we keep picking ourselves up, seeking Him, we can know joy in the midst of it. Better yet, God has designed an eternal home for us that not only offers justice but eliminates suffering completely!

Dear God, keep me teachable that I might grow up in you. Amen.

46

Beware!

Read 1 Peter 4:12-19

But to the degree that you share the sufferings of Christ, keep on rejoicing; so that also at the revelation of His glory, you may rejoice with exultation. —1 Peter 4:13

"Suffering is the quickest way to Christian maturity," Chuck Swindoll declares. It's true. When a crisis comes, priorities fall naturally into place. But when we tend to think our own sorrows are by far the deepest, we must keep in mind that everybody suffers.

BEWARE! Such an attitude can turn into a full-blown pity party, resulting in bitterness. As God does not measure sin, we should not measure suffering. I need to ask Him for compassion and insight that my experience may have purpose. When I can I reach out to others, for in reaching out I find healing within.

Heavenly Father, my scars are wide open today and the tears keep coming. Bind up my wounds with your love and remind me that my tears matter to you. Amen.

47

The Trap

Read Isaiah 14:3-10

> *Look and see if there is any pain like my pain*
> *which was severely dealt out to me.*
> *—Lamentations 1:12*

*O*ne midsummer evening I was taking pleasure visiting with friends over coffee and dessert. *Life is still beautiful,* I thought to myself savoring everything around me.

"Where did you say your daughter will be attending college?" my friend, Barbara, asked of her neighbor. "Way off in Illinois," she answered sadly. Tears caught in the corners of her eyes as she began giving us the details of how difficult this separation would be for her and her husband.

At least she's coming back! I wanted to shout at her. *"My Melanie's not!"*

I'm not even sure the woman knew of the loss of my daughters. But my evening was ruined, nevertheless, as I allowed the enemy to take over. Even though my situation was worse that mother still had a right to feel sad.

Satan finds many ways to snare us into pity parties. One of his sneakiest methods is to trap us into measuring the pain of others. Just as it is self-destructive to measure sin, it is equally unfruitful to measure grief.

Thank you, Lord, for your unending patience.
Help me to be compassionate to all your people. Amen.

48

Count Me Out

Read 1 Peter 4:12-19

But to the degree that you share the sufferings of Christ, keep on rejoicing; so that also at the revelation of His glory, you may rejoice with exultation. —1 Peter 4:13

*I*laughed heartily when I read Guindon's cartoon for the day. The instructor on television was about to present exercises to do while sitting down. The little old lady watching him sank down into her chair muttering, "Leave me alone."

Many times I feel just like that little lady. There are so many strenuous activities going on today, so many things we should do. Why should I choose to inflict more pain on myself when I am already suffering so much?

Such were my feelings a few years ago when our whole church decided to fast and pray for a brief time. I welcomed the prayer but resented the fast, grumbling and adding chicken broth garnished with croutons just to make the liquid diet bearable. Somehow I seem to think I am exempt from deliberate choices of suffering. I need all the comfort I can get!

One early morning, precisely in the middle of my prayers, a kind voice whispered, "Yes, Jan, you do know suffering, but not by choice. Would you choose it for Me?"

Dear Lord Jesus, thank you, for choosing to suffer for me. Help me to choose it for you. Amen.

49

A Change Of Attitude

Read Lamentations 1:10-14

*Is it nothing to all you who pass this way?
Look and see if there is any pain like my pain which
was severely dealt out to me.* —*Lamentations 1:12*

*S*o much of the time I think the pain that I live with is worse than anybody else's, and that nobody really understands what I go through. One exception to this feeling occurs when I am with my friends at the nursing home. Nevertheless, this passes and I enter my world of pain once more.

Last week I attended a quiet day at my church. The day consisted of total silence from early morning until late afternoon, including the lunch hour. Something awesome took place, something that seems to be changing my attitude.

Our pastor took us on a mental journey from the busy marketplace to a quiet sanctuary. The room was a mess—rubbish heaped into a corner, paper peeling away from the walls. Obviously, this room was seldom used.

Although quite unusual for me, I was able to be still enough to put myself into the scene that he was creating. Next he described the knocking on a door bolted from the inside. Finally, as the rusty bolt was pried open, a man entered the room. It was Jesus, wearing His crown of thorns. His face was full of agony. My pain grew more intense and I began to weep.

For a short period of time, *it was not my pain I felt, but that of Jesus!* And now I know, not just in my head, but in my heart, that no one suffers as does Jesus!

Dear Jesus, forgive my self-indulgence. Help me to focus on you. Amen.

50

A Dependency

Read Isaiah 26:1-6

*Trust in the Lord forever, for in God the Lord,
we have an everlasting Rock.* —Isaiah 26:4

I suffer with chronic physical pain. Like Paul, I've prayed for it to go away. But it remains.

In addition to T.M.J. (temporal mandibular joint syndrome) and arthritis in my upper arms, neck and shoulders, I have extensive surgical scar tissue in my pelvis. I have to carry around a donut of foam rubber to sit on in case I happen upon a wooden seat. I must be sure the donut is in my choir stall each Sunday before services, so I don't have to carry it during the processional.

Last summer I attended an elaborate wedding. The elegant reception was held on the lawn of the bride's parents' home. There I stood, all dressed up, among hundreds of people, with my canapes in one hand and my blue-covered cushion with the perky rooster on it in the other. It's embarrassing much of the time, but the alternative is far more painful than the embarrassment.

Although I don't like the pain or the cushion, they keep me dependent upon the Lord. Only He can ease the pain and take away the embarrassment. Dependence is productive when it is placed upon God!

Oh God of comfort, help me to look beyond the pain to you. Amen.

51

Giving

Read Matthew 25:34-46

For I was hungry, and you gave Me something to eat; I was thirsty, and you gave Me drink; I was a stranger, and you invited Me in . . . —Matthew 25:35

*M*y mother was a strong servant of God who shared everything she had. Because of my father's drinking problem, there was very little money to go around, yet she always managed to give something to others.

Often, hungry vagrants would come to our door. Sitting on the back steps, juggling a china plate and cloth napkin, they would dine on the best food she had.

Every Friday we looked forward to homebaked biscuits and caramel nut rolls. Our friends could hardly wait, knowing they would be invited. What little we had was shared.

"God sure blesses Mrs. Frykman's money," a neighbor once remarked. And He did, as she blessed Him with her time and attention, reading from her worn Swedish Bible, making prayer her stronghold—and ours. Not only did my mother give, she gave out of her own needs, and received the reward of her giving.

Dear Lord Jesus, thank you for my mother. Show me how to be as giving as she. Amen.

PART SIX
The Joy Of Obedience

52

My Father's Voice

Read John 12:3-8

> *Honor your father and your mother, that your days may be prolonged in the land which the Lord your God gives you.* —Exodus 20:12

*O*ne sunshiny summer morning, I was getting an early start on my weekly cleaning when the doorbell rang. "Hi, Dad," I greeted my father excitedly, "What a nice surprise!"

I wasn't quite so whipped-up when, over coffee, my father told me he had traveled sixty miles to see us so that the children and I could join him for a picnic and "a little fishing" at a nearby lake.

Because an immaculate home was a high priority for me, I argued, "That would be fun, Dad, but I can't just let my cleaning go."

Lovingly, my father turned and said, "Your house will always be here, Jan. But I won't."

When Mary used a whole pound of very costly perfume to tenderly anoint the feet of Jesus, Judas chided, "Why was this perfume not sold for three hundred denarii and given to the poor?"

Jesus commanded, "Let her alone, for the poor you always have with you, but you do not always have Me."

Dear Lord Jesus, remind me that sometimes listening is more important than doing. Amen.

53

Taking Time

Read Matthew 6:5-15

> *But you, when you pray, go into your inner room, and when you have shut your door, pray to your Father who is in secret, and your Father who sees in secret will repay you.* —Matthew 6:6

I haven't always rolled out of bed at 5:30 a.m. Before I entered into a personal relationship with Christ, I was definitely a night person. In fact, my husband teasingly called me "Moon Flower" because I blossomed when the sun went down.

In the wee hours, my head would fall upon the pillow and I would mumble a couple of brief prayers followed by "Our Father,"—a prayer which was rarely completed.

My friend Cathy helped me change all that. At our Tuesday morning prayer group, we were discussing the importance of taking time out each day to be with God. As usual, my excuse was concern for family and friends. My intentions were genuine, but many days I had so many interruptions there was no time left for the Lord.

Cathy, always convincing with her loving smile, shared, "That's why I don't take any chances, Jan. I have my prayers first thing in the morning."

Such a routine may not be right for everybody, but it has certainly been right for me. When I ask God early in the morning to protect my loved ones, He frees me of that worry. It's as though I have wrapped a blanket of Christ around them. Now, more than ever, I don't want to "take any chances with God."

I have heard that "Prayer makes God irresistible." I am beginning to discover the truth in that statement.

Father, I open myself to you. Keep me in constant communication by arranging my time with you daily. Amen.

54

Obedience Rewarded

Read 1 John 5:1-3

For this is the love of God, that we keep His commandments; and His commandments are not burdensome. —*1 John 5:3*

*I*t was Friday, my afternoon to lend a hand with the bingo game at the nursing home.

Although I usually looked forward to my time with these people I had grown to love, such wasn't the case today. I began to make excuses to justify not going: "My arms and neck are hurting and I really should rest. I'm so tired I won't be of much use."

But strictly out of obedience, I arrived at the nursing home, still murmuring under my breath. My spirits lifted a little when I set up the bingo game and the residents began to arrive. Who would not be touched with compassion at the sight of so many handicaps and so much pain?

Then my spirits nose-dived once more when I realized that I was the only ablebodied volunteer. "I knew I should have stayed home," I thought to myself. Everything seemed to be going wrong, and many of the residents appeared bossy and crabby.

When the game was finally over, I turned to go, eager to get to my car where I could scream and cry. But irresistible Dorothy called me back. "Jan," she said, blowing me a kiss, "I love you . . . forever and forever."

Lord, forgive my grumbling. Teach me to lose myself in others. Amen.

55

A Serious Matter

Read Matthew 5:38-48

But I say to you, love your enemies, and pray for those who persecute you.　　—Matthew 5:44

*A*s a small child in Sunday school, I first heard these words of Jesus. I suspect that I didn't think He was serious, or even that it was possible to "pray for your enemies." Not until I became an adult did I decide to take Him up on the challenge.

Having lived in our new home only a short time, Jim and I were excited to discover that new neighbors were moving in next door. When they arrived two weeks before Christmas, we rushed over to introduce ourselves, arms laden with firewood and freshly baked cookies. Our friendship developed over coffee and other social activities. Their small daughter and I became trusting friends— a relationship which her mother welcomed. Then came a misunderstanding!

Not only would the parents not speak to any member of our family but their daughter would quickly turn her head at the sight of me. At first I was hurt, then infuriated. But as time went by I became conditioned to the situation. Almost a year passed.

One day, while I was praying, my neighbors' faces popped into my mind. At the same time I was reminded of the verse I had learned in Sunday school so many years ago. Each day for several months I felt prompted to pray for that family, even though we still had absolutely no contact.

One morning the phone rang. "Hi, Jan," my neighbor greeted me warmly. "It's been such a long time. Could you please come over and have coffee with me on Wednesday?"

Dear Jesus, thank you for the miracle of healed relationships. Amen.

56

Out Of Order

Read Mark 3:31-35

For whoever does the will of God, he is My brother and sister and mother. —Mark 3:35

"*B*ake the snickerdoodles," the gentle voice seemed to say. But it was the holiday season, and I wasn't interested in wasting my time making an ordinary cookie.

My cupboards and my refrigerator were laden with walnuts and pecans and every colored baking candy imaginable. I had purchased sugared pineapples and cherries, and I had even bought currants to replace my more common raisins.

"Bake the snickerdoodles," the voice said again.

"I can't bake those drab cookies for Christmas," I argued. "Baking has to be fancy and showy for the Christmas season. I'd be embarrassed to serve snickerdoodles to my guests. They're not butter cookies. You always get out the butter for the holidays."

"Bake the snickerdoodles."

This time I began to listen. "But only my family likes snickerdoodles, Lord. I'm sure my company won't."

Oops, I thought. *Shouldn't my family come first?* Jim hated those fussy little cookies, and both Debbie and Jamie loved the cinnamon snickerdoodles.

With satisfaction and contentment I pulled out the huge yellow bowl and began stirring up my family's plain favorites.

I wonder how many blessings I've missed because I haven't listened to God's leading? I wonder how much turmoil I've caused when I could have had peace?

Forgive me, Lord, for my stubbornness. I want you to lead. Help me to follow, to keep my priorities in order. Amen.

57

A Prayer Reminder

Read Matthew 26:36-41

> *Jesus wept.*
>
> *—John 11:35*

"*I* have a gimmick," our pastor told us in a recent sermon, urging us to meet in prayer with God daily. His "gimmick" works as a steadfast reminder for him.

"When thoughts of skipping prayer arise," he said, "I picture a waiting Lord standing there with a look of disappointment on His face." I was reminded of my own selfishness with God.

Repeatedly, I describe my frustration and disappointments to Him with very little thought of His own similar feelings. Surely He is saddened when I make promises I fail to keep. And how many times does He receive leftover fruits rather than my first? How often do I grab at prayer answers and blessings with barely a "thank you"?

Upon the death of Lazarus both Martha and Mary chided Jesus with "Lord, if you had been here my brother would not have died."

When Mary and the consoling Jews began to weep, so did Jesus. "Behold how He loved him!" confessed the Jews. And He loves us as He did Lazarus—and waits for us to come to Him.

Dear God of love, forgive my selfishness. Help me to remember that you are a feeling Lord, and instill in me the desire to please you above all. Amen.

58

Your Glory, Lord, Not Mine

Read 2 Corinthians 4:1-6

> *For we do not preach ourselves, but Christ Jesus the Lord, and ourselves your servants for Jesus' sake.* —2 Corinthians 4:5

*M*any times, particularly in the past, I have found myself overwhelmed with the problems of others. As friends saw me work through a crisis, they often came to me during their own. Sometimes my heart would jump when the phone rang or the doorbell buzzed. I honestly cared about people, but I also feared I might go under myself.

The Savior asks us to share each other's burdens and put our own experience to work. But how can we accomplish that without falling apart ourselves?

Through prayer and evaluation, I discovered that I was often shouldering the problems alone by directing my friends to me rather than to Christ. I am learning to let go. As the burdens are given to Christ, so also is the glory.

Dear Lord, thank you for your willingness to shoulder all for my sake. Teach me to bring souls to you and not myself. Amen.

59

Clean Before God

Read Psalm 86

> *For Thou, Lord, art good, and ready to forgive.* —Psalm 86:5

"*I*'ve always liked Frankie," remarked my son Jamie about one of his close childhood friends. "I think the thing that made our relationship so good was that whenever we got into our little fights, one of us would phone the other to say that he was sorry."

Forgiveness doesn't always come that easily for adults. Sometimes we want to hang on to our anger a little longer, almost enjoying it. Besides, we rationalize, "Maybe that person needs to learn something from this."

But I learned from my relationship with Melanie the freedom of forgiveness. Forgiveness flowed continually between Melanie and me, and that freedom left me with fewer regrets.

When I finally put my anger to rest and come to a place of forgiveness, I always wonder why I waited so long. Nothing is more freeing or more cleansing than forgiving.

HAPPY ARE THE PEOPLE WHO FORGIVE, FOR FORGIVENESS IS A MIRACLE OF GOD!

Thank you, Lord Jesus, for making forgiveness possible. I love you. Amen.

60

Deserving Of Forgiveness

Read Matthew 18:21-35

Then Peter came and said to Him, "Lord, how often shall my brother sin against me and I forgive him? Up to seven times?"

Jesus said to him, "I do not say to you, up to seven times, but up to seventy times seven."

—*Matthew 18:21,22*

"*I*t's much easier to lose a child than it is to lose a husband," declared the voice on the telephone. It had been three months since Melanie's death, and I felt as though the caller was driving a sword through my stomach.

"I have lost two children," I retorted, "and I don't think you should make those kinds of remarks to people unless you have walked in their shoes."

I've always considered myself to be a very forgiving person. Complaining to the Lord one day about a particular situation, I reminded Him of my forgiving nature. Rambling on, I stopped short when I heard, "Yes, Jan, you are a very forgiving person . . . to the people who commit the same sins that you do!"

I remembered that caller, realizing that because I could never have made a remark such as hers, I felt she did not deserve my forgiveness.

But Jesus never said we were to forgive only those who deserved to be forgiven, but all people—not once but seventy times seven! If He has forgiven me, undeserving as I am, how much more should I forgive those who hurt me!

Father, forgive me for my judging smugness.
Thank you for always forgiving me. Amen.

61

More Than Once

Read Matthew 6:9-15

For if you forgive men for their transgressions, your heavenly Father will also forgive you. —*Matthew 6:14*

I was scheduled for surgery, a hysterectomy and bladder repair. I was reasonably calm about the operation as I looked forward to better health.

But following the surgery, I woke up in the recovery room with a peculiar feeling of weakness and pain, one that I had never experienced before, even though I had undergone other operations.

"What's wrong?" I questioned in a weak voice.

"There are a few complications," som.:one answered.

"Her blood pressure is very low," said someone else.

Doctors and nurses hurried by.

"Am I going to die?" I could barely speak.

"We are doing all we can." This time it was the doctor. When they couldn't get any blood pressure, Dr. R. looked down at me, saying, "I'm sorry, Mrs. Carpenter, but we have to take you back to surgery." I was unable to move a finger or to speak by the time they lifted me back onto the operating table. I could faintly hear the doctors shouting for more blood.

I was, indeed, close to death. "A suture somehow wrapped itself around one of your main arteries," Dr. R. informed me later. "You lost a lot of blood. If you want to blame someone, I guess it will have to be me."

Jim was livid. "How could you botch up the operation and let me sit all day, not knowing what was going on?" he demanded. Nine hours had passed from the time of my surgery until my arrival in intensive care, and although he had asked repeatedly no one had told Jim a word of my condition.

I found it difficult to be angry with Dr. R. He seemed willing to accept the blame, assuring us that there would be no charge for the second, exploratory operation.

But in a few weeks Dr. R. moved to another state, leaving Jim with the full bill and me with complications.

Forgiving Dr. R. the second time was not so easy. His acceptance of the blame and responsibility had given me a new faith in him. Then he walked out, billing us for *his* mistake. However, as Dr. James Dobson says, "Forgiveness is giving up my right to hurt someone who has hurt me." Such forgiveness is not easy, but it is vital for spiritual health and freedom.

Dear Lord Jesus, I choose to forgive, knowing that only then can you forgive me. Amen.

CONCLUSION
The Resurrection Song

62

A Little Girl's Lesson

Read Psalm 25:16-22

> *Turn to me and be gracious to me, for I am lonely and afflicted.* —*Psalm 25:16*

*N*inety-eight years separated the two figures squeezed together in the chair. Flora, a bright cheery lady who had just celebrated her one hundredth birthday held my beaming, enthusiastic granddaughter Carrie, who had just rounded birthday number two.

Carrie was accompanying me on my regular visit to the nursing home. She was enthralled with Flora as the elderly lady dramatically spoke of the mementos that filled her room. Later they shared cookies that Flora's daughter had baked.

Finally, exchanging goodbye hugs, Carrie and I left the room hand in hand. All of a sudden Carrie dropped my hand and ran back to the doorway of Flora's room. Peering around the corner she shouted, "BLESS YOU, FLORA!"

That little girl had sensed the loneliness in her new friend, and longed to leave her something to hang on to. Carrie didn't know she was demonstrating Jesus' love to Flora; she simply gave out of the abundance of her childlike love.

Heavenly Father, create in me a longing to care for others as you care for me. Amen.

63

Melanie's Easter

Read John 11:21-46

I am the resurrection and the life; he who believes in Me shall live even if he dies." —John 11:25

*N*ever has the power of resurrection been stronger in my life than at Melanie's death. Although hundreds of prayers had been offered for her recovery from the accidental brain injury, she died.

Only two years before, we had knelt together, hand in hand, as she accepted Christ as her Lord and Savior. Melanie had many difficulties placed before her, and yet her life was filled with activities. God had given her a genuine love and acceptance for all His people.

At our request, her funeral carried the theme of joy, overflowing with music and words of God's love and power. Our pastor referred to her death as "Melanie's Easter." This experience was probably the most trying of my life, yet I sensed peace and even joy through my tears as we sang together, "He shall raise him up . . ."

This joy lay in the knowledge that my child was in the presence of the almighty God. It was painful for the rest of us, but for Melanie it was Easter!

Thank you, Heavenly Father, for transforming ends into beginnings through the death and resurrection of your only begotten Son. Amen.

64

Majestic In Holiness

Read Exodus 15:11-13

Who is like Thee among the gods, O Lord?
Who is like Thee, majestic in holiness, awesome in
praises, working wonders? —*Exodus 15:11*

*M*y Lord, you are my COMFORTER. You not only soothe my sorrows but you also grant me joy in the midst of them.

You are also my best FRIEND. You walk hand in hand with me, and when I am feeling weak you pick me up and carry me.

You are my PHYSICIAN. You bind up my wounds and diminish my pain; you are the ultimate healer.

You are my ATTORNEY. You offer the best solutions possible, my Counselor and Advocate.

You are my DELIVERER. You reach down and pluck me out of the pit, setting my feet upon the solid rock.

You are my loving FATHER. You cradle me in your arms, tenderly wiping away all my tears.

You are my LAMB of God. You take away all my sins.

You are my SAVIOR. You offer me eternal life and the blessed promise of a reunion with Jody and Melanie!

You are my CREATOR. You give me life. Without you, I would not be.

I humbly bow before you in adoration, my majestic KING OF KINGS, my LORD OF LORDS. Who am I that I should be loved by you? Yet you are to me all I need you to be. Thank you, Father. Amen.

65

All Because Of Him

Read Philippians 4:4-19

> . . . *for I have learned to be content in whatever circumstances I am.* —*Philippians 4:11*

I used to count on the future to provide my happiness. Because my expectations were high, I was often disappointed. Then came Jesus!

He taught me to live in the *NOW*. *Now*, the positive traits about people stand out. *Now*, I like myself, even though I know I make mistakes. *Now*, I can experience today's pleasures, instead of counting on tomorrow's.

Sometimes it's still an effort to get up in the morning, but I am eager to see what He has planned for me each day. He can make sending a note to a shut-in as thrilling as attending a dinner in my honor.

I am beginning to understand what Paul meant when he said he had learned to be content in all circumstances. I can even see the possibility of singing praises in a cold dank prison.

A few months ago, I received recognition for my service on the board of directors at our church. I received a gift and a large pink button with a picture of piano keys and the words, "Jesus put the song in my heart." I keep it pinned above my desk where I can always see it, so that I will never forget who gives me my song.

The extent of victory we receive over our grief, or any other hardship, is in direct proportion to the measure of our lives that we are willing to surrender to Christ. The deeper the suffering, the greater the joy; the greater our joy, the more powerful the testimony!

Thank you, Lord Jesus, for turning sorrow into SONG! Amen.

66

Simple But Crucial

Read Romans 10

> For "whoever calls upon the name of the Lord will be saved." —Romans 10:13

*M*y father lay dying, his body riddled with cancer. He could no longer use his voice, so he spoke by moving his eyes and shaking his head. The pain was so intense that he thrashed about and had to be bound to his bed.

Our time together had been short. And although he was an alcoholic for most of my life, I had always found him easy to love and easy to forgive. In the past ten years he had remained sober, and, we had become very close. He thought that I was perfect, and though I knew better, his opinion made me feel good.

When I looked at him again, so sick and so weak, I could not hope for him to live. Cold fear charged through me as I thought of his death. "Where does he stand with the Lord? I think he believes, but . . ."

I tried to compose myself as I read him the twenty-third psalm. When I looked up, I saw huge tears filling the corners of his eyes. "Dad," I questioned hopefully, "would you like me to call a minister to come and visit you?" He responded quickly with a clear nod, this time the tears spilling over his face.

After my Dad's death, I worried about his salvation. One day, years later, God assured me that my father had taken Jesus into his heart when he genuinely, and without hesitation, nodded *Yes*.

I believed in God for over forty years, yet I struggled desperately. I attended church regularly but did now know what it meant to be born again, or that a personal relationship with Jesus was even possible.

I am convinced that I could not have made it through these last few years without that relationship. There is no comparison between enduring Jody's death—believing but powerless—and my acceptance of Melanie's death—believing and charged with resurrection power. Such power is available to anyone who chooses to accept and follow

Jesus Christ. When I surrendered my life to Christ, I prayed a prayer similar to this one:

Dear Lord, I know that I am a sinner.
Please forgive me.
Come and live in my heart.
Be the Lord of my life.
Thank you, Jesus. Amen.

Paul gives us this assurance: "If you confess with your mouth the Lord Jesus and believe in your heart that God has raised Him from the dead, you will be saved."

Romans 10:9

Lord Jesus, thank you for changing my life and restoring me to yourself. Let my life demonstrate your love to others. Amen.